SAINTS ALIVE!

Andy Robb

Copyright © John Hunt Publishing Ltd
46A West Street, Alresford, Hants SO24 9AU, UK
Tel: +44 (0) 1962 736880 Fax: +44 (0) 1962 736881
E-mail: office@johnhunt-publishing.com
www.johnhunt-publishing.com

Text © 2003 Andy Robb
Illustrations © 2003 Andy Robb
Design by Nautilus Design, UK
Page layout by Andy Robb

ISBN 1 84298 124 2

Scriptures quoted from the Good News Bible published by The Bible
Societies/HarperCollins Publishers Ltd., UK

A CIP catalogue record for this book is available from the British Library.

Printed in Singapore by TWP

CONTENTS

It might come as a bit of a surprise to you but *some* people think that being a Christian is just for **wimps**.

It *doesn't*? Oh well, at least you're on the ball with what people think about things.

Anyway, in *some* people's book (we're talking about a *pretend* book here) being a Christian is about as exciting as **arranging flowers** or **collecting postage stamps** ...

As far as *they're* concerned, going to **church** is best left to old ladies and babies (not forgetting people who collect postage stamps) ...

Which is a bit odd, to say the very least, because if you check out the *Bible* then you'll soon discover that this couldn't be *further* from the truth!

Just to prove it, here's the lowdown on a few people from the Bible who **followed Jesus** (which is *another* way of saying they were **Christians** but we like to broaden your vocabulary in the Boring Bible books – aren't we good?).

Name: Paul.
What Happened To Him: Imprisoned (loads of times), whipped (loads of times), close to death (loads of times), had 39 lashes (five times – which was *still* loads), stoned (just the once), shipwrecked (three times), been in danger from floods, robbers, enemies in the wild!

Name: James.
What Happened To Him: Put to death by the sword!

Name: Stephen.
What Happened To Him: Stoned to death!

Name: Peter.
What Happened To Him: Whipped and imprisoned!

Now correct me if I'm wrong, but what *those* four guys had to endure for being a Christian could hardly be called '**wimpish**', could it?

In fact, I'd go as far to say that it's probably about as far *removed* from flower arranging and stamp collecting as you could possibly get.

THAT'S IT! I'VE HAD ENOUGH! WHY DON'T YOU GO AND PICK ON SOMEONE ELSE FOR A CHANGE?

And if you don't believe me then here's what *Jesus* said about people who wanted to follow him ...

IF ANYONE WANTS TO BE ONE OF MY FOLLOWERS HE MUST STOP PUTTING HIMSELF FIRST AND BE PREPARED FOR THINGS TO GET TOUGH.

The Bible doesn't *quite* put it like that, but it's pretty much what Jesus meant.

Just in case you're wondering, Jesus wasn't trying to put people *off* becoming Christians, he was simply letting us know (loud and clear) that ... **it isn't for wimps!**

Making Jesus **No.1** in your life means you're on *God's* side and you've now got *him* to take care of you.

But it also means that you're now *working* for him, doing what *he* wants.

He's the **Boss**!

Being a Christian means that you've become one of God's **agents.** Now that's what I call *exciting* ...

EVEN MORE EXCITING THAN COLLECTING POSTAGE STAMPS?

Yep, astounding though it may seem, even *more* exciting than *that*!

Being an **agent of God** (which is what *this* book's all about) means that you're gonna need a bit of **beefing up** to get yourself into shape *before* we let you loose on the world.

This Boring Bible book is your very own **agent of God training manual** and it's jam-packed *full* of stuff that's gonna make you into a tip-top follower of Jesus.

And if you're wondering *why* this Boring Bible book is called '*Saints Alive!*' then you'll just have to wait a little bit *longer* to find out.

All will be revealed at the right time 'cos as every *good* agent knows, all **important info** must only be passed on when we can be absolutely *certain* that nobody's listening in!

MOST FRUSTRATING! WE WILL HAVE TO BE PATIENT UNTIL THIS GREAT SECRET OF OUR ENEMY IS REVEALED, AGENT X!

MESSAGE RECEIVED, AGENT Z!

Anyway, if you're up for it (getting trained up as an agent of God) then turn the page and get stuck into your first **Agent Briefing**.

AGENT BRIEFING NUMBER ONE:
CHURCH FACT FILE

Don't let the title put you off! If you're gonna be a supa-dupa **agent of God** you've gotta check out all the data on the organisation that you're working for. If you were a **CIA** or **MI5 agent** then you'd need to have a jolly good idea *how* the whole organisation ticked and *why* it had actually started in the *first* place. So get back to your desks and continue with your training. We're not having any of this picking and choosing lark. **It's all or nothing!**

HEY, THAT'S NOT A PROBLEM? I STUDY ANCIENT HISTORY EVERY DAY – MEET MY PARENTS!

Now if you've if you've managed to get round to reading Boring Bible book *Hyper Holy Happenings* (on sale in all good bookshops – and maybe even in some not *quite*-so-good bookshops) then you'll be up to speed on *everything* to do with how the church got kick-started.

But just for those of you who *haven't* had the chance to spend all their hard-saved pocket money (yet!) on that *particular* book, here's the **potted version**.

The whole *point* of **Jesus** visiting planet earth was to take the **punishment** for all the wrong stuff we do that stops us being friends with God and then showing us *how* we could live lives that really *pleased* God.

To do that we needed God to come and live *inside* of us so, (after Jesus had gone back home to heaven), he sent his **Holy Spirit** to do just that (if we were up for it).

The people Jesus had left behind were the first in line to get this brilliant gift from God and it revolutionised their lives.

One minute they were more than a little bit scared of admitting that they had anything to do with Jesus and the *next* they were suddenly **unstoppable**, **power-packed** agents of God who simply *couldn't* shut up about Jesus.

Not only that but as they started to do miracles (like healing people) loads *more* of the people in **Jerusalem** (where they were hanging out) became believers in Jesus and joined forces with them.

In fact, before they knew it there were *thousands* of them and it seemed like it wasn't going to stop *there*.

And *that's* really how the **church** got started.

Now it's probably a good idea if we clear up a little bit of confusion early on just in case you're not *completely* sure what exactly the church *is*.

You have two choices and here they are ...

Choice a)

Choice b)

So, *which* one's the church?

Yep, you were right (unless you were *wrong*) it's **choice b)**

Although there are heaps of very pretty (and some not-so-pretty) church buildings all *over* the place they're not actually what the Bible *means* when it talks about the church.

What it means is all the **Christians** - which is why **choice b)** was correct. The church is like one **great big team** of people (all round the world) who've made *Jesus* **No.1** in their lives.

Got that? Good! Let's keep moving.

Fascinating Fact: *It's been estimated that roughly 1.6 billion people around the world would say that they're Christians – which is an awful long way from the few hundred that followed Jesus while he was alive.*

Now here's something that *every* **agent of God** needs to know and it's this.

God's got an enemy.

Ah, yes, but we're not not talking about *people* here, we're talking about someone called **the Devil**. Ever since he was chucked out of heaven he's been doing his level best to turn everyone *else* against God as *well*. The Bible says you're either on *God's* side or you're *not* - and if Jesus *isn't* **No.1** in your life then the Devil will do his *utmost* to make you give followers of Jesus a hard time. And that's *exactly* what started happening to those guys (and gals) who were there at the start of the church...

... but they didn't!

So they started getting beaten, tortured, thrown into prison and *even* **killed**. The battle was on.

Every **agent of God** had become a target for the Devil and he was using his *own* human agents to do his dirty work.

Keep your agent notebooks open and your pens poised because (as you'll very soon discover) God's enemy was planning to do everything he *could* to disrupt God's plan to use the church to tell the world about Jesus.

But it wasn't *all* bad news.

Thanks to the **Romans** (and their new network of roads that stretched all across that part of the world) those first Christians could travel easily with the good news that Jesus had given us a second chance with God.

Before you knew it there were church buildings and church groups all *over* the place.

It wasn't long before news about this Jesus reached even the ears of **Caesar** in **Rome**. Christianity was spreading like **wildfire**.

What had started as a small bunch of believers was growing into something massive and there seemed to be no stopping it.

Or *was* there?

We've already had a look at what the Romans were like in some of the *other* Boring Bible books and there's one thing we discovered that was *guaranteed* to really annoy them and that was **people who didn't do what they were told**.

Not *quite* what I was thinking of.
More along the lines of...

Hmm, well you can't argue with *that*, can you?

Whoops-a-daisy!

It looks like *some* of the Christians just aren't gonna play ball.

They weren't gonna stop worshipping Jesus just to please their Roman masters.

It was showdown time or should I say **showtime**!

Emperor Nero (who gets a mention in Boring Bible book *Hyper Holy Happenings*) had the world's biggest ego and the refusal of Christians to be good citizens of Rome (by bowing down to the Roman gods) **really riled him**.

Things came to a head when most of Rome was destroyed by a terrible fire and Nero laid the blame squarely (but unfairly) at the feet of the Christians ...

IT MUST HAVE BEEN THEM! WHO ELSE WOULD DO SUCH A DESPICABLE THING?

That's because many of his *not-so-loyal* subjects were suggesting that *he'd* done it because he wanted Rome to be **rebuilt**!

Nero set about using any Christian he could lay his evil hands on as entertainment in the **Colosseum** (a huge arena in Rome). For public entertainment, Christians were **mauled to death** by lions (and other things too gory to mention in *this* book).

It wasn't long before Christians had become **public enemy number one**.

Everyone seemed to hate them.

From now on it wasn't safe for these early **agents of God** to meet openly – Emperor Nero had driven Jesus's followers **underground**!

And when I say underground, I *mean*, underground!
Outside of Rome lay the **catacombs**, a vast network of
underground corridors
where the bodies of dead
Romans were buried.
The thought of burying
their dead in the actual *city*
was abhorrent to these
orderly (and superstitious)
people.

OOPS! I DON'T THINK I SHOULD HAVE BURIED MY PET GOLDFISH IN THE BACK YARD!

As for the Christians, well
they didn't have *any* hang-
ups about being near to
dead bodies, in fact Jesus
had taken *away* the fear of death from them.
So the catacombs seemed the *perfect* place to meet without
being hassled by the Romans.

Fascinating Fact:

**There are at least 35 different catacombs and someone
with nothing better to do has estimated that If you
put them end to end (which you couldn't do)
they'd make a total
of approximately 500 miles in length.**

You can still visit the catacombs today and scan the ancient walls
to see some of the inscriptions written by these first Christians.
To be fair to the Romans, they didn't all feel *quite* so strongly
about the Christians as Emperor Nero. *Some* just thought they
were the '**scum of the earth**' and that was the end of it. But
being an **agent of God** still wasn't for wimps. Check out this
story about a guy called **Ignatius** ...

Mauled to Death!

Ignatius had been around while some of Jesus's disciples were still alive and he'd been the main man (the bishop if you really want to know) in the church at Antioch.

(Antioch's where Christians first got *nicknamed* '**Christians**'.)

Ignatius had been in the hot seat for about 40 years when the Roman emperor (Trajan) paid a visit to the place. Trajan hadn't got time for these followers of Jesus and promptly had poor old Ignatius arrested and chained up ready to be shipped off to Rome to be served up to the lions.

How would *you* feel if that happened to you?

Calm down now!

Now let's see what doomed *Ignatius* had to say for himself ...

Er, not *exactly* the sort of response we were expecting, eh?
Ignatius was getting on a bit and the long trip by land and sea
was gruelling, particularly as it was approaching winter.
To *add* to his suffering, the soldiers accompanying him treated
him cruelly. But Ignatius was *not* the sort of **agent of God** to be
downcast by such an ordeal. He even used the time he had
while travelling to write to churches encouraging them not to
give in to the enemy but to **stand firm for Jesus** ...

By the time he reached Rome the place was **buzzing** that this
important bishop was in town.
It was the last day of the games (and just before Christmas) and
the amphitheatre was *packed* with Romans itching to see our
hero torn **limb from limb** by wild beasts.
Just to make *sure* he didn't slip through the net, Ignatius was
swiftly whisked into the arena and mauled to death for the
pleasure of the waiting audience. All that was left of him were a
few bones but Ignatius had already said that no way did he
expect to get let off the hook and to die like this for God was
an honour.
So, as you can see, working for God (against the enemy) is
certainly *not* for **cowards**!

Boring Bible Interesting Info:

Before Jesus was executed, he met with his disciples to have a meal.

He drank some **red wine** and said that it represented his **blood** that was very soon going to flow from his body as he became the world's perfect sacrifice for horrible sin.

Then he used the **bread** they were eating to tell them that it represented his **body** which he was allowing to be punished for our sin and its horrid side-effects.

Jesus rounded the whole thing up by saying that this *wasn't* just a **one-off meal** – they (and *all* believers) should carry on doing this as a handy reminder of Jesus's amazing sacrifice for us.

Unfortunately for those Christians living in the ancient Roman empire, some rather unhelpful rumours had started to do the rounds that these followers of Jesus were only meeting in secret because they were **drinking human blood** and worse, they were **killing children as sacrifices** to their God.

God's enemy, the Devil, was having a field day stirring up outrageous (and completely untrue) propaganda to set everyone against the Christians.

To see how hated they'd become, check out this bit of graffiti that was discovered on the wall of a house in Palatine Hill, Rome .,,

Alexamonos worships his god

Nothing odd about that but read on to find out what sort of picture was *with* it.

If anybody ever says that Jesus wasn't a *real* person then they'd better think again, 'cos the people in the first and second centuries sure believed he was. They were *forever* making references to Jesus (though not often very nice ones!).

That bit of Roman graffiti had a picture to go with it of Jesus hanging from a cross (like he did) but with an **ass's head** instead of a human one.

So, as you can see, if people weren't *killing* Christians they were making the most of taking the *mick* out of them

Now here's a question for you.

Why did everybody seem to have it *in* for the Christians?

YEAH, 'COS BEING A CHRISTIAN IS ALL ABOUT LOVING GOD AND OTHERS, ISN'T IT? NOTHING WRONG WITH THAT!

Too right, but there were a *couple* of things that about these Christians that really made people **hot under the collar**.

1) *They* believed what God had told them – that every human being has done wrong against God (sinned) so that *everybody* needs to say sorry to God and to cut out sinning in future.

2) *They* believed that there was only **one** way to heaven and that was by saying "**yes**" to Jesus being **No.1** in your life – you couldn't worship whichever god *you* wanted and *still* get into heaven when you died.

So *that* ruled out all the other gods and stuff that people worshipped which, as far as they were concerned, was just **a bit much**.

Who did these Christians think they were, going round telling people that sort of stuff? **How dare they!**

And the Devil definitely didn't like it (as we've already said). The last thing *he* needed was everybody to start worshipping **Jesus** and to stop worshipping **him** and his *so-called* gods.

But it wasn't all bad news.

Despite all this stuff going on, Jesus's church was **booming**. In fact business was brilliant!

By the time the *next* Roman emperor we're featuring (**Constantine**) came on the scene there were agents of God as far afield as **India**, **Arabia** and **Scotland** ...

Emperor Constantine was the first Roman ruler to really get stuck into this Christianity stuff though he probably didn't get it *completely* right. Nevertheless, around **AD300** (give or take the odd decade or two) he started to throw his weight behind the church until it actually became **acceptable** to believe in Jesus.

In fact, it was the people who *didn't* become Christians who were given a hard time.

With the *emperor* calling the shots it meant there were **good jobs** and **government positions** for people who signed up for Jesus. The trouble is, with the pressure *off*, Christians started to let things slip. Being a Christian was now a cushy little number with no chance of being **dish of the day** for hungry lions ...

People were becoming Christians just so they could land themselves a good job or a nice home.

To make matters *worse* **Emperor Charlemagne** (500-ish years later) carried things on and went to war against people who *weren't* Christians, forcing them to believe in Jesus – **or be killed!**

Once again the enemy had used *his* agents to infiltrate the ranks of the *true* Christians and bring about **confusion**. There was only one thing for it. They had to

agree on *what* Christians actually believed and then write it down for all to see. *That* way it would soon be clear who *was* and who *wasn't* the real thing.

Which is why (to his *credit)* Emperor Constantine took the bull by the horns and in **AD325** he assembled **318 bishops** from across the empire under one roof and got them to agree on what a Christian really *was*.

And they did.

For your info (and as we've said, **info** is what **agents** need) it was called the '**Apostles' Creed**' and we *still* use it today in the twenty-first century.

So that's a *quick* look at how the organisation you're an agent of (if you're a Christian) began to grow.

Sad, to say, the Roman empire began to **fizzle out** ...

... but not *before* there was a whopping great **falling out**.

Instead of there being *one* main city where the church had its HQ, there were now *two* – and *both* claimed to be the main one! The **Roman Catholic Church** had its HQ in Rome and the **Eastern Orthodox Church** had its HQ in Constantinople.

Added to which their leaders (or **popes** as they were called) became as **powerful** as kings. Some *even* had their own armies to help them become even *more* powerful than they already *were*.

Not *everyone* liked the way Jesus's church was heading (and I'm sure *Jesus* would be one of them) so let me introduce you to some guys who decided to turn their backs on it all and lock themselves away from the whole wide world.

Monk-y Business!

Monks were a bunch of guys who'd had just about enough of people using the excuse of making out that they were serving *God* just so as they could get what they wanted.

These monks went completely the *other* way and lived **poor and lonely lives** away from the rest of the world as they tried their very best to live good lives but *without* the temptations of money and power.

On the *plus* side they did manage to be a good influence on the world around them ...

... but on the *down* side, well, this was *hardly* the **full** and **joyful** sort of life Jesus had lined up for Christians.

So, by all accounts (after a really good start) the church had not turned out *quite* so well as might have been expected.

Okay, so the church had managed to set up **outposts** over *most* parts of the civilised world but, often as not, it didn't really bear much resemblance to the sort of thing *Jesus* started way back in **Jerusalem**.

On the *one* hand you had these powerful popes and other church leaders using their authority to **kill** or **victimise** *anyone* who didn't believe what *they* believed, and on the other hand you had people who thought that being a Christian meant trying their very best *not* to enjoy their lives for **fear of displeasing God**.

It looked like the church was **heading for destruction** and with it, everything Jesus had *ever* planned for the world.

Not so fast!

Okay, so God's agents had made a bit of a mess of **The Organisation** and had even allowed *enemy* agents to infiltrate its ranks, but when it boiled down to it Jesus was *still* **The Boss**, and *he* still had all the power of heaven at *his* fingertips.

Jesus's *church* might have lost the plot but Jesus *hadn't*, and it was time to bring that back on course.

Boring Bible Apology: Because this book's only got 128 pages we haven't got space to tell you every *teensy weensy* bit of info about the church through the centuries, so you'll just have to take it as read that loads of stuff happened.

Okay, if *that's* the way you want it, let's take it year by year. We should be through in a few months ...

A wise decision.

So basically, the church spread and grew in much the same way until about **AD1500-ish** when a German monk called **Martin Luther** stepped onto the stage ...

He'd been reading his **Bible** (as you would expect an agent of God to do) and had discovered from his investigations that the Pope wasn't getting things quite right.

So what was he doing, you might well ask?

Here's what.

The Pope was telling people that all they had to do to have their sins forgiven was to **stump up some cash** (to the church in Rome) and, **bingo!** their sins were forgiven.

Sounds a good money-spinner to me but Martin Luther decided to stick his neck on the line and point out that this was **wrong**. Oh dear!

Martin Luther announced (very publicly) that it was only *Jesus* who could forgive sins and *that* was the end of the matter.
He *then* added a whole list of *other* things he thought that the church was getting wrong and that were different to what it said in the Bible.
For his efforts Martin Luther was kicked out of the church ...

Not only had *Martin Luther* been ejected from the church but it seemed like Jesus's teachings had as well.
But all was not lost!
Our disgruntled German monk wasn't alone in coming to the conclusion that the church had rather **lost the plot** – loads of *other* people had as well.
And so started what was called the '**Protestant**' church.
(That's because they were *protesting* about wrong things being taught – what an education these Boring Bible books are).

Boring Bible Interesting Info: Loads of the churches you see around nowadays are Protestant churches including Methodist, Lutheran, Presbyterian, Episcopal, Baptist, Pentecostal and many more besides.

But that's not *quite* the end of the story – there's a few more bits of data that *every* **agent of God** needs to download.
And here they are.

Counter Offensive!

Over the next few hundred years, God's agents started to **mobilise**. At long last, the Bible had been translated from Latin into everyday **English** so that *everyone* could read what God had to say. (Up until then it was usually just church leaders who had access to the Bible).

Christians were starting to take being being a follower of Jesus seriously. In fact they were popping up far and wide showing people God's love and telling them that they could be friends with the God who'd made them.

Er, not quite *that* far and wide!

Places like China and Africa (plus heaps of others) were targeted by **agents of God**.

And Jesus's Organisation was beginning to influence the countries it had outposts in.

Christians worked their socks off to counteract the work of God's enemy (which was to make life unbearable) by starting **schools** and **hospitals** and by fighting *against* things like **slavery** and **poverty**.

At last Jesus's church was making the sort of mark that Jesus had *intended*!

Now cast your mind back to the *start* of this Agent Briefing to how those *first* **agents of God** became power-packed (it's on page 11 if you *really* can't remember).

DON'T TELL ME! IT'S ON THE TIP OF MY TONGUE...

What, like saliva?

GOT IT! IT'S THE HOLY SPIRIT, ISN'T IT?

Correct!

And the **Holy Spirit** was someone who most of the church had just about *forgotten*.

But not for long.

Over the last hundred years or so **agents of God** around the world have begun to *rediscover* the amazing power that God puts inside them when they become Christians.

And it's not *just* for adults – **kids** of *your* age are doing all the *same* sorts of **healings** and **miracles** that Jesus did because they're making full use of *his* power – which is what *every* **agent of God** (and that includes you, if you're one) is meant to do.

And *that*, in a nutshell, is **the history of the church**.

So now you know!

How very true!

Fascinating Fact:

Someone with time on his (or her) hands to do clever calculations has estimated that there are roughly 22,000 varieties of Christian denominations (names or styles of churches like Methodists and Baptists) in the world – at the last count.

Right, all you **agents of God** out there, time to hit you with our *next* top secret Agent Briefing. I hope you weren't banking on taking a break, 'cos time's short and there's work to be done!

AGENT BRIEFING NUMBER TWO:
AGENT OUTPOSTS

If you've been paying attention (which I'm sure you have 'cos you're an *excellent* **agent of God**) then you'll remember what we said about Jesus's church *not* being buildings but all his followers lumped together. Having said that, most Christians still actually meet up in buildings and guess what they get called? Yep, you guessed it ... **churches!**
How confusing is *that*?

What they really are is just **outposts** for God's kingdom.
(God's kingdom simply means everything that lets *Jesus* be its king – easy, eh?)
Now, there are **three sorts of people** who are reading this book (well there's actually *heaps* more but you'll soon see what I'm getting at!).

First off there's the person who's never, ever **set foot inside** a church building (or Agent Outpost) ...

If that's *you* then you've probably not the **foggiest idea** what goes on inside its walls.

The *second* sort of person is someone who's maybe been to something like a christening, a wedding or even a funeral (but hopefully not yours!) in a church. But *despite* that you *still* don't really have **a clue** (other than christenings, weddings and funerals) what on *earth* goes on in the place ...

Hmm!?

And the *last* sort of person is someone who's well and truly stuck into what's happening at their local church ...

So what we're gonna do in *this* Agent Briefing is fill you in on some of the stuff that you might (or might not) know about a **typical Agent Outpost**.

The *first* thing you're gonna need to know is *why* **agents of God** meet together in the first place.

Any ideas?

Not even close!
Let me put you straight.
As you all know by now,
God's enemy (the Devil)
is out to trip up any
agent of God he can
get his hands on ...

You can quit blubbing 'cos the *Bible* says that when we sign up as one of God's agents then *his* part of the bargain is to **protect us**.

But just like in *any* war, you can't just go off and do your own thing. You'll get picked off by **enemy sniper**s in *no* time.

You've gotta stick close to people who are on your side.

You've gotta work out tactics *together* so you can catch the enemy unawares.

You've gotta have people looking *out* for you as well as *you* looking out for them.

You've gotta *encourage* agents who are having a tough time so that you all stay fighting fit.

So, church is like an **agent of God** meet-up place where you get fired up for serving **The Boss**.

Another very good question.

So turn the page and check out a handful of **agent files** we've pulled out for you to investigate.

SINGING SONGS

You'd be forgiven for thinking that you could only *ever* be an agent of God if you had a thing about **singing** – after all, don't they sing loads of hymns? Yep, and other songs as well. Why? Well it's not because Christians like singing (although some do) but that they like to **sing to God** with songs of praise and worship.

SERMONS

If you wanna *really* make a go of being an agent of God then you're gonna need to know *loads* of mega important stuff about God such as what God's like, what he says is *good* and what he says *isn't*, how we can trust him and how we can know him more (for starters). Sermons (or preaching) is the church's name for being taught this sort of stuff.

COLLECTION

During *most* church services there's what's called a **collection** (or offering) where fancy bags or plates are passed round for people to drop money into. This isn't because God's hard up but it's a sort of way of saying that you're putting your **money where you mouth is** and want to give all you have to God. The money never actually makes it to heaven – it's used to pay for all the vital work each Agent Outpost has to do.

PRAYING

Being an agent of God means you can **communicate with HQ** (pray to God in heaven) whenever you want, but sometimes it's good to do it with the rest of the team.

That's why many Agent Outposts give **top priority** to praying about things: for example – for the people in their town, their friends and families, the sick, the government – you name it, the church prays for it.

That's just a quick glance at *some* of the stuff that churches get up to, but there's loads *more* on top of that.

Because they're outposts for God's kingdom they do all sorts of activities that show the people living nearby that **God loves them** and has got time for them.

Some churches run kids' clubs and youth groups.

Others do stuff for old people, young mums, people who're hurting, sick people, homeless people and out of work people.

You can't *force* people to become Christians (like some of those Roman emperors tried to do) but you *can* show them that God loves them by taking time out with them and caring for them.

In fact, God's agents are meant to care for people exactly like Jesus did when he visited planet earth.

Fascinating Fact:

The Bible says that the church is more than just an organisation – it's actually the body of Jesus Christ. That's because Jesus is in heaven now so he can't physically do the things he did while he was to-ing and fro-ing across the land of Israel. So, with the Holy Spirit inside us, we can represent Jesus, doing the same sort of things that he used to do – just like his body would have done!

So that's about it for **Agent Outposts** but just *before* you move on, here's a useful bit of agent info ...

Boring Bible Interesting Info: Christians meet up in church on *Sunday* because *Sunday* was the day that Jesus was raised back to life after being executed.

Aren't you glad you know that?

AGENT BRIEFING NUMBER THREE:
AGENT POWER

One thing's for sure, the church was never meant to do its stuff without **God's power** to make it work.

Imagine having an electric lawnmower and *then* not plugging it into the electricity supply ...

I WONDERED WHY IT HAD TAKEN ME THREE WEEKS JUST TO CUT THIS LITTLE PATCH OF GRASS!

Likewise, **God's agents** need **power** if they're gonna have *any* sort of success in what they do.

How do you *get* that power?

Easy! Ask God. When you sign up to join forces with Jesus the **Holy Spirit** comes to live inside of you but it doesn't stop *there*. You've gotta *keep* plugged into your power supply by asking the Holy Spirit for more.

If you're not sure then let's check out the secret of *Jesus's* success.

After all, it's *him* we're following, so whatever *he* did then so should *we*!

SUPER MAN!

JESUS HAD JUST BEEN REVEALED AS GOD'S SON AND NOW HE HAD WORK TO DO...

JESUS WAS LED OUT IN THE DESERT BY THE HOLY SPIRIT TO GET HIM READY FOR HIS MISSION...

THE DEVIL TRIED TO TEMPT HIM TO JACK IT ALL IN BUT JESUS STOOD FIRM...

From that moment on, Jesus set about **healing the sick**, giving evil spirits their **marching orders** and even bringing dead people **back to life**.

Not only *that* but when Jesus taught people about God they hung on his *every* word, because what he said sounded like it came from the mouth of someone who had some sort of **authority** to say it.

Which brings you to the conclusion that if *Jesus* (who was God's very own Son) needed to be **power-packed** with the **Holy Spirit** to send the enemy packing and to reintroduce the world to God, then *every* other **agent of God** does as *well*!

Okay, so that's *why* you need God's power – now let's check out what exactly you *get*.

Your Agent Power Pack

Let's suppose you're out and about, minding your own business, when ...

Yikes! Sounds scary! But 'cos you're **power-packed** with the Holy Spirit, not *only* can you *pray* for sick people but you can also *expect them* to get well – just like *Jesus* did!
Or what if something like *this* happened ...

What you're definitely gonna need is something called **wisdom** and **discernment** which is the Holy Spirit's way of telling you what *is* (and *isn't*) good for you.

Or then again what if ...

What you're gonna need is real **boldness** to tell it like it is *without* being worried about what anyone thinks of you. And that's something that only the **Holy Spirit** can give you. There's lots of *other* reasons for being filled with God's power but these *three* will at least help you to realise that no **agent of God** can *ever* go it alone (without God's power).

But being power-packed with the Holy Spirit of God is only half the story ...

The *other* of part of the Holy Spirit's work is to help us be **more and more like Jesus**, which sounds a really tall order but, as you're about to find out, *nothing's* impossible for **your Boss**.

Fruity Facts!

I'll bet you like getting **prezzies**, like at Christmas or on your birthday. **Me too!** Well, when it comes to doling out goodies, the Holy Spirit's *way* out in front of the rest of us. Being the generous God that he is, God *specialises* in giving us **good things**. Not *only* does the Holy Spirit give us all the abilities we've just checked out on the previous pages (the Bible calls them '**gifts of the Spirit**') but he's *also* in the **fruit distribution business**.

HE'S NOT ALONE!

But the fruit that *God* deals in is all **100% quality produce**. Let me explain.

When the Holy Spirit takes up residence in an **agent of God** that's not the end of it – there's now **work** to be done!

WORK? I THOUGHT THAT ONCE I'D SIGNED UP FOR GOD THAT WAS THE END OF IT!

Er, I'm afraid not. That's just the *start* of it.

When you got your call-up papers to sign up as an agent for **The Organisation** (God's Kingdom) then I'll bet you checked out what you were letting yourself in for *before* you came on board. And there are a couple of important things you should have been told (or found out).

The First Important Fact: Signing up to be an **agent of God** means you're in line to get loads of good stuff (including the gifts of the Spirit) from God.

The Second Important Fact: Signing up to be an **agent of God** means *you've* gotta line up with *God* – which means he expects *you* to become more and more like *him*.

Before you start to get too fretful and worry how on *earth* you're gonna do that, ease up!

That's what this **fruit business** is all about. With the Holy Spirit living inside of you, God is able to change *all* your bad ways and habits to make you more and more like *him*.

How does he do that? Simple – it's teamwork.

Your job is to let the Holy Spirit do his stuff and then *he'll* do the rest.

Okay, so it's not gonna be an *overnight* thing but God's never been into quick fixes – so that's alright then.

The Bible calls this the '**Fruit of the Spirit**' 'cos it's like God is **growing good things** inside us.

And just in case you were wondering what *exactly* God's like (so that you can become more like him) here's some of the 'fruit' that the Bible tells us God wants to produce in **you** ...

So, there you have it.

If you're gonna **cut it** as one of God's agents then be *sure* to collaborate with the Holy Spirit. That's all part of God's brilliant plan for making his church effective.

Lots of **power** – and *lots* of **fruit**.

Boring Bible Interesting Info: If you want to impress your parents (or any other grown-up of your choice) with how *spiritual* you are then tell them that you are being 'sanctified' by God. '**Sanctification**' is the big word that's used to describe all that fruity business we've just had a look at.

Boring Bible Agent Jokes

Agent: "Doctor, doctor, I can't understand this secret message."
Doctor: "I wouldn't worry about it. It just sounds like you've got a very bad **code**!"

What do agents eat at Christmas?
Mince spies!

What do you get if you cross James Bond with Father Christmas?
Ho Ho Seven!

Boss: "Agent 006.5! Why are you still in bed when you should be at work?"
Agent: "That's 'cos I'm an **undercover** agent, sir!"

AGENT BRIEFING NUMBER FOUR:
COMMUNICATING WITH HQ

Okay, so far, so good. We've had a look at what the church is all about and how **Agent Outposts** go about their business.

And we've looked into how you can be a **power-packed agent of God** and how you can be *more* like Jesus, your boss.

So, *already* you can start to see that being a Christian is about the *least* **wimpish** thing you could *ever* imagine. Being an **agent of God** means you've gotta be *serious* about belonging to God's organisation.

Now, if you've ever seen any films about secret agents you'll know *all* about how when they're out on their missions they make a point of **calling up their HQ** (headquarters) to check out *what* to do next and to tell HQ *how* things are going.

Guess what? Agents of God can do the very *same* thing but *we* call it '**praying**'.

Praying is simply communicating with *your* HQ (**God in heaven**) to find out what *he* wants *you* to do and to keep him up to date with how you're doing.

Nothing complicated in that, is there?

I DON'T KNOW ABOUT THAT! TRYING TO PUT YOUR HANDS TOGETHER, CLOSE YOUR EYES AND PRAY, ALL AT THE SAME TIME — SEEMS A BIT TRICKY TO ME!

Despite that, *most* agents of God still find praying **hard to do**.
And I'm now gonna tell you *why*.

But just in *case* there's any **enemy agents** lurking, I think we'll
reveal *this* **top secret info** behind closed doors ...

 **TOP SECRET**

Right, here goes. The reason *most* **agents of God** find praying a big deal is that God's enemy (the Devil) is doing his very best to thwart them.

THAT'S DAFT! HOW CAN HE STOP YOU PRAYING?

Well he can, but not in the sort of ways you'd **expect**. God's enemy is a very *devious* character so you need to stay **alert**. Check out some of his **underhand methods** to *stop* you communicating with HQ.

Underhand Method One:

YAWN! I'VE SUDDENLY COME OVER ALL SLEEPY! I THINK I'LL GIVE PRAYING A MISS!

That's God's enemy at work trying to make you feel **sleepy**!

Underhand Method Two:

No prizes for guessing who sent your mates round *just* when you were about to pray? Okay, so that might not be the case *every* time but you still need to be **alert**!

Underhand Method Three:

Who wants you to feel that praying is about the **dullest** thing you can ever think of? Yep, you got it. God's enemy (and yours), **the Devil**!

So what're you gonna do about all this **enemy interference**? If you let him get *away* with all his sly tactics then *he's* won.

Here's the plan – but keep it hush hush.

In fact, just to make *certain* that no enemy agents get wind of what I'm about to tell you, the message you're about to read is not only upside down – it's back to front as well.

(Hold it up to a mirror). Here's the plan ...

If you're gonna make a habit of communicating with HQ then you're gonna have to be **really determined**. Don't let yourself be sidetracked – stick with it.

That's what being an **agent of God** is all about.

Boring Bible Top Tip: One way of making *sure* you stick with sending through your communication to God is by joining forces with other agents and praying together. *That* way you can encourage each other.

Simple! The Devil knows full well that once the lines of communication are *opened* then there's absolutely **zilch** that he can do to *stop* that prayer reaching God.

Your prayer to God is like a **missile** (but without any explosives in it!) which you aim at heaven and which God's enemy can't stop 'cos he hasn't *got* any **anti-prayer** missiles to shoot it down with.

How to Pray

in three easy lessons

First Easy Lesson:

Pray with *faith*. That means when you ask God for something you've gotta really *believe* that he's going to give you *what* you're asking for. Which means you're gonna have to get to know God so *well* that you can **trust him completely**. And if you want to be sure that you're asking for the *right things* then

spending a bit of time reading a Bible might be a good idea. The Bible's *packed* with bits that give you big clues about what God *does* (and *doesn't*) want to give us. Asking God for things definitely *isn't* like writing an 'I want ...' list for **Santa Claus**!

Second Easy Lesson:

If you want to get your prayers heard *and* answered then you need to make sure you're *not* doing things that God says you

shouldn't (which the Bible calls '**sin**'). Before you even *start* down the road of asking God for things you've gotta say "**sorry**" to him for being *out* of line and commit yourself to staying *in* line from then on.

Third Easy Lesson:

If you want God to do something for *you* then you've gotta do something for *him* first. And that's to forgive anyone you've got a grudge against. Why's *that* you may ask? It's because *God* went out on a limb to forgive *you*. So long as you refuse to forgive anyone (for anything) then the line's dead for answers to your prayers.

Hmm!? Perhaps with a *little* more feeling!

Make a **decision** (*whatever* you feel about someone) to forgive them, just like *God* forgave *you* – *then* you can start expecting those prayers **to get answers**.

Just before we round up this Agent Briefing let me leave you with a fistful of other handy tips to get the most out of communicating with HQ.

Don't keep **waffling on** to God about nothing in particular. You won't get a better result by rabbiting on more. **Get to the point!**

Kick *off* your time talking to God by just **thanking him** for all the things he's done for you. Then howzabout **praising him** for all his good qualities – tell him what a *great* God he is. In no time at all you'll stop just thinking about *yourself* and instead you'll have your **sights locked on to God**. Before you know it, some of the things that were worrying about won't even seem *half* so scary, or maybe you'll have a lot more confidence that God can answer your prayers. Either way, it's a good idea to **do it**!

And last, but not least, why not use *some* of your airtime with God, not for *talking*, but for **listening**. If you're chatting to a friend then it would be a bit of a one way conversation if only *one* of you did *all* the talking. There's *loads* of things God wants to say to you and some of it might even be the answers to your prayers. So high priority should be given to **mouth shut – ears open**. Not sure how to hear from God? Don't worry! The more time you spend with God the

easier it'll become to hear *what* he's saying. Often as not it'll be something like a **thought** popping into your head and the chances are that's *God* talking to you. Exciting, eh?

AGENT BRIEFING NUMBER FIVE:
SPILLING THE BEANS

Being an **agent of God** isn't the *same* as being a **secret agent**. There are no secrets with God. All the information you have downloaded about Jesus is ready and waiting to be passed on to anybody who'll listen.

This information is called the '**good news**' because that's *precisely* what it is. It's *good* news that Jesus has sorted out the world's **sin problem** and made it possible for us to get back to being friends with God. And *that's* the info that **agents of God** have got the task of **broadcasting**.

Jesus never intended for us to keep **tight-lipped** about what he'd done for the world. Here's what Jesus told his disciples way back nearly 2000 years ago ...

GO THEN TO ALL PEOPLES EVERYWHERE AND MAKE THEM MY DISCIPLES. BAPTIZE THEM IN THE NAME OF THE FATHER, THE SON AND THE HOLY SPIRIT AND TEACH THEM TO OBEY EVERYTHING I HAVE COMMANDED YOU.

Not only *that* but Jesus told them (and *all* agents of God) that they'd be like a **lamp shining brightly** for *everyone* to see. So Christians can't lurk in the shadows hoping that nobody'll notice them. You've gotta be out there so *everybody* can **see** you and so they can **hear** what you have to say.

CAN'T I JUST LURK IN THE SHADOWS A TEENSY BIT?

Not only *that* but Jesus said we've gotta be like **salt** to the world – *without* salt things become **tasteless** and **rotten**. It was like Jesus was telling his followers that they had to put *back* some of **God's flavour** into his world and to stop it going *rotten*.

Listen up, young **agent of God**. Time to see how you're gonna **spill the beans** about Jesus.(That means tell it to everyone).

As you can see, you don't *have* to stand on a street corner and
shout to all the world everything you know about Jesus.
Every day you get *plenty* of opportunities not only to *tell* people
that you're a Christian (and why) but to **show** it as well.
Just like the girl in the comic strip, every **agent of God** has a
choice whether to *do* or *say* something – **or not!**

So start to look out for **agent opportunities**. And don't worry
what to say or *do* – don't forget that you've got the **Holy Spirit**
giving you *all* the help you'll *ever* need.

Boring Bible Top Tip:
Don't forget to communicate with God about all of this.
Ask *him* for opportunities to tell people about Jesus or to show
people his love. And you can **pray** that your friends or family
will *also* become God's agents.

Right, young agents of God, before you get stuck into your *next* **Agent Briefing** we're going to check out some really important stuff for you to download and store. So here goes.

For your info, there are **two** sorts of agents:

The *first* sort of agent is one who is always **one step behind the action**. They're always getting caught unawares and spend half their time just getting themselves out of trouble.

This sort of agent is unprepared – and an **unprepared** agent is an **ineffective** agent!

But the *second* sort of agent is one who is *always* prepared – come what may.

So, how're you gonna shape yourself into an **agent of God** who's always prepared? Let me fill you in.

If you want to be always on the ball, ready for action then you need to line yourself up with **what God says**.

What do I mean by that?

Simple! The Bible (which is called **God's Word** 'cos it contains the *words* that *he* spoke) is packed with loads of brilliant stuff that tells you what God thinks of you, what he's done for you, what he wants to do for you and what he's given you to help you make a go of being an agent of God.

Your job is to **lock** onto to them, **download** them and **hang on** to them. *That* way, when things get a bit tricky or tough, then all *you've* gotta do is remind yourself of what God has to say on the matter.

That way you won't be one of those **up-and-down** sort of agents who seems to spend *most* of their time just trying to **survive**.

Okay, so God doesn't *mind* us crying out to him when we're in difficulty, but there are *some* tricky situations that we could avoid in the **first place** if we just kept on board with God by holding on to his words.

And here are some of them that you need to download ...

God's Words to Hang on to!

And we've personalised them from *God* to *you*. Kind or what?

> IF I AM FOR YOU, WHO CAN BE AGAINST YOU?

> YOU ARE HOLY AND DEARLY LOVED BECAUSE I HAVE CHOSEN YOU.

> I WILL NEVER LEAVE YOU OR ABANDON YOU.

> LEAVE ALL YOUR WORRIES WITH ME BECAUSE I CARE FOR YOU.

> I HAVE LOVED YOU WITH AN EVERLASTING LOVE.

> YOU ARE A NEW CREATION IN JESUS CHRIST. THE OLD HAS GONE - THE NEW HAS COME.

> YOU CAN DO ALL THINGS THROUGH CHRIST WHO GIVES YOU STRENGTH.

That's just for starters. The Bible's **jam-packed full** of stuff that God wants you to listen up to (and remember) so that you'll know just how *precious* you are to him, how much he *loves* you and how much he wants to *do* for you – if only you'll just keep on **trusting him**.

WARNING!WARNING!WARNING!

God's enemy the Devil specialises in trying to whisper lies into the ears of any unsuspecting agents of God who'll hear him. He'll do *everything* in his power to make them believe that God *doesn't* love them and that they can't *really* expect God to look after them. Our Boring Bible advice is this: **Don't listen to him!**

Boring Bible Top Tip: Read the Bible bits from the previous page **out loud** to yourself and **memorise** them so that you really start to *believe* them, Before you know it you'll be thinking about yourself like *God* thinks about you – and *that* means you're almost *guaranteed* to be a **better agent of God**.

And don't just take *my* word for it. Do a bit of special agent investigating of your *own* and see if *you* can uncover some helpful Bible bits yourself which you can **read out and learn**.

AGENT BRIEFING NUMBER SIX:

GIVING CREDIT TO GOD

If you're anything like *me* then I'll bet that your **ears prick up** when somebody says something **nice** about you ...

There, what did I tell you! It works *every* time.

But (so the Bible tells us) having nice things said to us is not a **one-way street**. Okay, so God wants to let us know what *he* thinks of *us* (as we've just seen) but this is a **two-sided coin**. (Sorry about all the metaphors but you've gotta take the **rough with the smooth** – oops, there I go *again*!). As an **agent of God**, you're also expected to give some **credit** (or praise) *back* to your Boss and Master.

Not got a *clue* what praising God is about? Read on!

Credit, Where Credit's Due!

Let's suppose for one *wild* moment that someone **really important** or **famous** turns up in the front room of your house, such as...

Or perhaps...

As you can see, we find it almost impossible to *stop* ourselves lavishing praise on big-shot people (not that most of us actually get to *meet* any, but that's not the point) so, how about aiming a bit of the action in *God's* direction?

Well, for starters, **God is more important** than even the most *important* person in the world.

Yep, even more important than *you*, chum!
In fact, let's do a quick run down of a few of the things that make God important.

What Makes God Important

1) Well, first off, God was around *way* before the likes of you and me. The Bible quite helpfully informs us that not *only* has God been on the scene for longer than even your mum and dad but that **he's been around for ever**. There's *never* been a time when God *hasn't* been God – which rather puts in the shade even the most *important* person that's ever set foot on planet earth.

2) A*nother* thing that shouldn't be overlooked is that God is in *charge* of everything. Every successful business has a **boss** and **Universe Incorporated** is no exception. So, not only does the buck stop with God but also *he's* running the show so (to put it bluntly) what **God says goes** and there's the end of it.

3) If God hadn't made planet earth (and for that matter you and me) then we wouldn't be even *thinking* about this stuff. The whole whopping great universe was **God's idea** down to the most insignificant little creepy crawly ...

... so I figure that we should be more than just a little bit **grateful to God**, don't you?

4) God is **awesomely powerful** and **holy** which means that if you were suddenly catapulted into his presence at this very moment then you would be completely overwhelmed with his **greatness** (and your **weakness**). Check out the Bible and you'll very soon discover that in heaven (where God lives) everyone is *forever* falling down before God in worship. Not only that but whenever even one of God's *angels* makes himself known to a human being then – **bam!** – whoever he's appearing to falls flat on their face or is filled with fear.

5) But, before you get *too* hung up about thinking you're gonna have to try and avoid God at all costs for fear of being anywhere *near* someone so **amazing and big** – ease up! The *good news* is that God is also a God of **mercy** and **love**. That means that he *isn't* out to get you. For your info, it's the complete *reverse*. God's *so* keen for us to be in his presence that he sent Jesus down to planet earth to give us the opportunity. Phew! *That's* a relief. It's just that God wants us to treat him with the **respect** and **honour** that he deserves and if we are up to speed with what God is actually *like* than that shouldn't be a problem, should it?

Good, so here's some handy **agent of God** ways to get started praising God. If you're up for it then let's get cracking!

Now, if you didn't know already, the Bible's *stuffed* with bits about **giving credit to God** (praise and worship) for *who* he *is*. If you've read Boring Bible book *Catastrophic Kings* (as recommended by my kids – I'll have to up their allowance now) then you'll know all about the **Psalms** (pronounced 'sarms').

BIT OF A WASTE OF TIME BUNGING A 'P' AT THE BEGINNING THEN, ISN'T IT!?

Most of these brilliant Bible bits were written by a guy called **King David** who really appreciated who God was and wanted to make sure he told him.

We're gonna nick a few of David's ideas to get ourselves up and running and then maybe come up with some of our *own* afterwards.

How do you give credit to God? The same way you would to *any* important person ...

I THINK YOU'RE WONDERFUL!

AW! SHUCKS!

...you **tell** them!

So, young agent of God, tune your vocal chords, find yourself somewhere private ...

... well, perhaps not *that* private – and then get stuck into **praising God** by reading out these psalms.

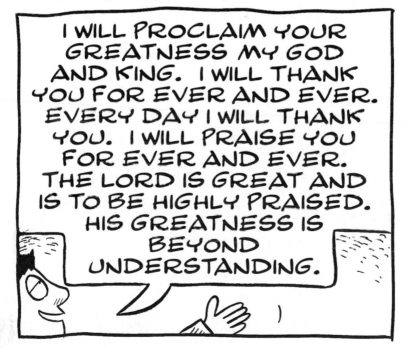

(A snippet from **Psalm 145**, **verses 1** through to **3**)

Or how about giving *this* one a go ...

THE LORD IS GREAT AND
IS TO BE HIGHLY
PRAISED. HE IS
HONOURED MORE THAN
ALL THE GODS. THE
GODS OF ALL THE
NATIONS ARE IDOLS BUT
THE LORD CREATED THE
HEAVENS.
GLORY AND MAJESTY
SURROUND HIM.
POWER AND BEAUTY FILL
HIS TEMPLE.
PRAISE THE LORD ALL
THE EARTH.
PRAISE HIS GLORY AND
MIGHT.
PRAISE THE LORD'S
GLORIOUS NAME.

This one's from **Psalm 96** and using **verses 4** to **8**.

And last, but by no means least, the first **five** verses of
Psalm 33 ...

ALL YOU THAT ARE RIGHTEOUS SHOUT FOR JOY FOR WHAT THE LORD HAS DONE. PRAISE HIM ALL YOU THAT OBEY HIM. GIVE THANKS TO THE LORD WITH HARPS. SING TO HIM WITH STRINGED INSTRUMENTS.
SING A NEW SONG TO HIM. PLAY THE HARP WITH SKILL AND SHOUT FOR JOY! THE WORDS OF THE LORD ARE TRUE AND ALL HIS WORKS ARE DEPENDABLE. THE LORD LOVES WHAT IS RIGHTEOUS AND JUST. HIS CONSTANT LOVE FILLS THE EARTH.

So, as you can see, this giving credit to God business is not only
essential for all **agents of God** but it's also **fun**, and often very
noisy (which should appeal to *most* of you!).

Agent of God Info:

You might not know this but the *more* you **praise God** the *more* you become aware that **he is there**. In fact the Bible tells us that God *inhabits* the praises of his people (that's every agent of God). That means the *more* you give credit to God the *more* he'll let you experience his presence. But don't just take *my* word for it – **try it yourself**. And make sure that you don't short-change God by only giving him a *couple* of minutes of your time. If you're really, *really* serious about this **agent of God** stuff then how about giving God **five** or **ten** or even **twenty minutes** of your time ...

It might *well* be, but if you wanna be an **effective agent** then you've gotta decide *where* your priorities lie ...

And just before we close *this* **Agent Briefing** here's one last bit of advice. There's one thing that *every* **agent of God** should *always* have with them and it's *this* ...

AN ATTITUDE OF GRATITUDE!

Wherever you go, *whatever* you do, always keep yourself primed and ready to **give thanks to God** for what he's doing in your life. Which brings *this* **Agent Briefing** to an end.

Right, here's your chance to have put your **agent skills** to the test. Check out the **Boring Bible Codecracker** and *then* use it to *decode* some of the brilliant codes that the **Boring Bible Code Department** (well, that's just me, actually) has specially devised for you.

Don't worry, they're not hard – I wouldn't have been able to think them up if they *were*!

Okay, that's the **Codecracker**. Just in case you hadn't quite twigged how it works let me fill you in.

If I set you a code like *this* ,..

ZTVMG

... all you've gotta do is look along the **Codecracker** to find white code letter 'Z' and to see what letter is above it which in this case is the letter 'A'. *Next* up is white code letter 'T' which is below the a 'G' and so on until you've decoded the word 'AGENT'. Easy peasy! Off you go with the *rest* of the Codecrackers.

Codecracker One:

R ZN GSV ERMV ZMW BLF ZIV GSV

YIZMXSVH. DSLVEVI IVNZRMH RM NV

ZMW R RM SRN DROO YVZI NFXS UIFRG.

Bible book John chapter 15 and verse 5

(Write your solution in the white boxes)

Codecracker Two:

DSVM ZMBLMV RH QLRMVW GL

XSIRHG SV RH Z MVD YVRMT.

GSV LOW RH TLMV, GSV MVD SZH XLNV.

Bible book 2 Corinthians chapter 5 and verse 17

Codecracker Three:

RG RH YB TLWH TIZXV GSZG BLF SZEV

YVVM HZEVW GSILFTS UZRGS.RG RH MLG

GSV IVHFOG LU BLFI LDM VUULIGH.

Bible book Ephesians chapter 2 and verses 8 and 9

Codecracker Four:

GL SZEV UZRGS RH GL YV HFIV LU GSV

GSRMTH DV SLKV ULI, GL YV XVIGZRM

LU GSV GSRMTH DV XZMMLG HVV.

Bible book Hebrews chapter 11 and verse 1

AGENT BRIEFING NUMBER SEVEN:
BIBLE BASHING

Just like any *other* sort of special agent, **agents of God** have got their very *own* **agent manual**. Your agent manual is where you gen up on all the background of the organisation that you're working for and download all the **vital info** that you're gonna need to carry out your missions *properly*. Christians call *their* agent manual '**The Bible**' and it's an absolute *must* for every agent of God to understand.

If you want *loads* of stuff about the Bible then get your hands on a copy of Boring Bible book *Bible Buster*. For now, we thought it would be useful to give you a quick rundown some of the main info. But first ...

Fascinating Fact:

The Bible is consistently the world's best-selling book and someone with a lot of time on their hands has worked out that between 1815 and 1975, 2.5 billion Bibles were printed. The best-selling versions are the King James Version, the New International Version and the Living Bible.

Put simply, the Bible is a book full of stuff that God wants us to know which is why it's often called God's '**Word**' 'cos it's what *he* wants to say.

Let's take a speedy look at what some of those things are.

One of the *obvious* things that the Bible tells us is that there really *is* a God.

Although the whole of God's wonderful creation (the universe, the world, animals, plants, people) all seem to shout out loud and clear that there's a God who thought it all up and lovingly pieced it all together, loads of people *still* can't see it, even though it's **right in front of their eyes** ...

So the *Bible* is there to make it *plain* to them ...

The Bible *also* tells us **what God is like**.

It would be no good having a boss (if you worked) who you didn't have the *foggiest* idea about. You wouldn't know *where* you were. So God uses the Bible to fill us in on some details about himself (*our* Boss). To keep you up to scratch as an agent I'm going to give you them in **code** so you can flick back a few pages to the **Codecracker** and use it to decode *these* not-too-taxing brainteasers ...

Did you notice sometime *interesting* about the **third** word in that code? If not have *another* glance.

Answer: It uses the same letters coded *and* decoded.

Just in case you didn't *quite* manage to solve them all I've decided to be kind and put the answers at the bottom of the page. If you want to get the *full* picture about what God's like then you'll have to get stuck into the Bible yourself to make a few valuable discoveries of your **own**. Anyway, let's keep moving with this **Agent Briefing**.

God is merciful. God is holy.
Codecracker answers: God is love. God is faithful.

Another thing that the Bible reveals is that God's got an **amazing plan** for human beings. According to the Bible, we're not all just **freaks of nature** that have evolved from swamp life or from some **gassy explosion** in outer space. In fact, so the *Bible* tells us, we're not *even* related to **apes** like some people would have you believe ...

The Bible is quite clear that you and I have got a **purpose** and God has got a **plan** for not *only* the whole world but each of our lives as well – but more of *that* later.

So, what you get when you take a look in the Bible is heaps of info about *how* God made the world, *why* God made the world and how it was always his plan for us to be **friends with him** and to **enjoy his company**. Okay, so things have gone wrong, but that doesn't mean that God's *plan* has changed. **No way!** If you want the *full* story then Boring Bible book *Crazy Christians* is the one to read, but for now it's important to download the fact that **God's interested in you and me – big time.**

What's *brilliant* about the Bible is that it not *only* tells you how things were at the very *beginning* of time and how the world got up and running but it *also* fills you in on how the story *ends*. Just about everything you ever needed to know about life, the universe and God is **jam-packed** into this *one* book.

Well, *almost* everything, okay!

So that's why it's **imperative** (very important) that *all* **agents of God** start to investigate the Bible for *themselves*.

To give you a bit of a helping hand we've lined up a few Boring Bible investigations just to get you going.

But *before* you do, check out the following info which you're gonna need to download into your memory banks so you can do your **undercover investigations** *properly*.

BORING BIBLE
Bible Investigation Check List

1) You're gonna need a Bible (obvious but true!).

2) You're gonna need to know how a Bible works. **Here's how:** The Bible's made up of **66 separate books** starting with **Genesis** and ending up in **Revelation**. Each book is divided up into **chapters** (just like any other book would be). And then each chapter is divided up into **verses** (the non-rhyming variety).

So, if I tell you to look up **Genesis chapter 7** and **verse 6** all you've gotta do is head for Bible book Genesis, skip along until you find chapter 6 and then run your finger down the page until you find verse 6 (in teensy lettering). Easy, eh?

3) Before you *start* reading the Bible your best bet is to **communicate with HQ** (pray) to check out what **message** God wants you to get out of the Bible bit you're about to investigate.

4) Oh, yes! Find somewhere **quiet**. The *last* thing an **agent of God** needs is to be *distracted*.

Right, now off you go and get your teeth stuck into these juicy **Bitesize Bible Investigations** and we'll rendezvous again once you've finished them.

(Just in case you don't own a Bible we've printed all the Bible stuff out in full – how kind is that?)

I'M LOST FOR WORDS!

Bitesize Bible Investigation: Operation Jerusalem

Bible Bit Location: Mark chapter 11, verse 1 through to 10.

'As they approached Jerusalem near the towns of Bethphage and Bethany they came to the Mount of Olives. Jesus sent two of his disciples on ahead with these instructions ...

GO TO THE VILLAGE THERE AHEAD OF YOU. AS SOON AS YOU GET THERE YOU WILL FIND A COLT TIED UP THAT HAS NEVER BEEN RIDDEN. UNTIE IT AND BRING IT HERE. AND IF SOMEONE ASKS YOU WHY YOU ARE DOING THAT, TELL THEM THAT THE MASTER NEEDS IT AND WILL SEND IT BACK AT ONCE.

So they went and found a colt out in the street, tied to the door of a house. As they were untying it some of the bystanders asked them "What are you doing untying the colt?"
They answered just as Jesus had told them and the men let them go. They threw cloaks over the animal and Jesus got on. Many people spread their cloaks on the road while others cut branches in the fields and spread them on the road. The people who were in front and those who followed began to shout, "Praise God! God bless him who comes in the name of the Lord! God bless the coming kingdom of King David, our father! Praise God!"'

Background info: Jesus was heading into Jerusalem knowing full well that he would very soon be arrested and executed. Up until then he'd criss-crossed the land of Israel telling people that he was going to make it possible for them to be friends again with God (and proving it by doing loads of amazing miracles). *This* Bible bit is like the build-up to the big finale.

Some questions for you: Why do you think Jesus picked a **colt** (sometimes referred to as a donkey) to make his grand entrance into Jerusalem? I mean, this is God's one and only **Son** we're talking about! Write your answer here ...

  I think Jesus rode into Jerusalem on a colt because:

Here's another question.
If you'd been in that crowd of people do you think *you'd* have been one of those people that were **praising Jesus?** If your answer's "Yes!", then *why*?

  I'd be praising Jesus because:

Great stuff! Are you ready for your *next* **Bible Investigation**? Good, then let's keep rolling!

Bitesize Bible Investigation: Temple Turmoil

Bible Bit Location: Mark chapter 11, verse 15 through to 18.

'When they arrived in Jerusalem, Jesus went to the Temple and began to drive out all those who were buying and selling. He overturned the tables of the money-changers and the stools of those who sold pigeons and and he would not let them carry anything through the temple courtyards. He taught the people...

The chief priests and the teachers of the Law heard of this, so they began looking for some way to kill Jesus. They were afraid of him because the whole crowd was amazed at his teaching.'

Background info: The Temple in Jerusalem was where the Israelites worshipped God. It was *also* the place where they made sacrifices to God. It had become a big business selling the animals that were to be used for this purpose. Not only that but the Temple only accepted special currency for the gifts the people were expected to make, so all the Israelites' cash had to be changed up. And *that* was good news for the money-changers who were ripping the people off something rotten.

One *more* thing. The chief priests and teachers of the Law were using their power to give the Israelites a hard time and had made following God into a terrible burden.

Some questions for you: Why do you think Jesus caused such mayhem in the Temple?

I think Jesus did what he did in the Temple because:

And one more question to think about ...
Why do you think the religious leaders wanted to kill Jesus?

I think the chief priests wanted Jesus dead because:

Bitesize Bible Investigation: Jesus's Last Meal

Bible Bit Location: Mark chapter 14, verses 17 through to 26.

'When it was evening, Jesus came with the twelve disciples.
While they were at the table eating, Jesus said "I tell you that
one of you will betray me – one who is eating with me."
The disciples were upset and began to ask him, one after the
other, "Surely you don't mean me, do you?"
Jesus answered, "It will be one of you twelve, one who dips his
bread in the dish with me. The Son of Man will die as the
scriptures say he will but how terrible for that man who betrays
the Son of Man! It would be better for that man if he had never
been born!"
While they were eating, Jesus took a piece of bread, gave a
prayer of thanks, broke it and gave it to his disciples ...

Then he took a cup, gave thanks to God and handed it to them
and they all drank from it.

Jesus said ...

THIS IS MY BLOOD WHICH IS POURED OUT FOR MANY, MY BLOOD WHICH SEALS GOD'S COVENANT. I TELL YOU, I WILL NEVER AGAIN DRINK THIS WINE UNTIL THE DAY I DRINK THE NEW WINE IN THE KINGDOM OF GOD.

Then they sang a hymn and went out to the Mount of Olives.'

Background info: This was Jesus's *last* meal with his twelve disciples (followers) before he was executed – and *Jesus* knew it. The meal they had was actually called the '**Passover**' meal and the Jewish (or Israelite) people used it to remember when God's angel **passed over** (and avoided) their homes when they were slaves in Egypt but killed all the firstborn Egyptians (as a punishment for treating the Israelites so badly). God told the Israelites to daub lambs' blood around the door frames of their houses so that when the angel came by he would pass over and not cause harm. Jesus was using the red wine from this meal to say that *his* blood was soon going to be shed so that God wouldn't punish *us* for all our wrong-doing.

And the bread Jesus used to represent his body that was shortly to be killed.

Some questions for you: Have a think why any of Jesus's twelve disciples would want to betray him into the hands of the religious leaders (who wanted him dead). Do you think that one of them had never really *understood* why Jesus had come to earth in the *first* place? Or perhaps someone thought that Jesus wasn't *quite* the great leader he'd hoped?

I think that someone wanted to betray Jesus because:

And what would *you* have said to Jesus when he hinted that he was about to allow himself to be killed?

When Jesus suggested that he was about to allow himself to be killed I would have ...

Bitesize Bible Investigation: The Trial

Bible Bit Location: Mark chapter 15, verse 6 through to 15.

'At every Passover Festival Pilate was in the habit of setting free any one prisoner the people asked for. At that time a man named Barabbas was in prison with the rebels who had committed murder in the riot. When the crowd gathered and began to ask Pilate for the usual favour, he asked them "Do you want me to set free for you the king of the Jews?"
He knew very well that the chief priests had handed Jesus over to him because they were jealous.
But the chief priests stirred up the crowd to ask, instead, for Pilate to set Barabbas free for them.
Pilate spoke again to the crowd ...

"But what crime has he committed?" Pilate asked.

They shouted all the louder, "Crucify him!"

Pilate wanted to please the crowd so he set Barabbas free for them. Then he had Jesus whipped and handed him over to be crucified.'

Background info: Jesus had been arrested after he'd gone to the Mount of Olives with his disciples. The religious leaders were trying to convict Jesus on the grounds that he claimed to be the Son of God (which he *was* but *they* didn't believe it). The Roman governor, a guy called Pontius Pilate, was a bit confused by it all and didn't quite know what to do with this Jesus who had been handed over to him.

After all, he hadn't broken one single Roman law – unlike that hardened criminal Barabbas.

Some questions for you: Why do you think the crowd suddenly turned against Jesus?

 I think the crowd turned against Jesus because:

And why do you think that Jesus didn't try to persuade Pilate that he was being **set up** by the religious leaders?

 I think Jesus kept quiet because:

Bitesize Bible Investigation: Mission Accomplished

Bible Bit Location: Mark chapter 15, verse 33 through to 39.

'At noon the whole country was covered with darkness which lasted for three hours. At three o'clock Jesus cried out with a loud shout ...

... which means, "My God, my God, why did you abandon me?" Some of the people there heard him and said, "Listen, he is calling for Elijah!"

One of them ran up with a sponge, soaked it in cheap wine and put it on the end of a stick. Then he held it up to Jesus' lips and said, "Wait! Let us see if Elijah is coming to bring him down from the cross!"

With a loud cry Jesus died.

The curtain hanging in the Temple was torn in two from top to bottom. The army officer standing there in front of Jesus saw how Jesus had died. "This man really was the Son of God!" he said.'

Background info: Jesus had been sentenced to death by
Pontius Pilate and then taken away to be whipped and beaten
as a preparation for being nailed to a wooden cross (which was
the Romans' cruellest form of execution).

What *nobody* realised was that this was all part of God's plan to
get the whole human race back to being friends again with God.
God needed a perfect sacrifice to take the punishment for all the
world's sin (wrong-doing). And *Jesus* was just about to finish the
job of *being* that sacrifice!

Some questions for you: Why do you think that Jesus shouted
out that God had abandonded him? A big clue is that *our* sin
has the effect of separating *us* from God.

 I think that Jesus felt abandoned because:

And that army officer. What do you think he saw in Jesus that
made him say that he thought Jesus was the Son of God?

 I think the army officer saw in Jesus:

Bitesize Bible Investigation: Back To Life

Bible Bit Location: Mark chapter 16, verse 1 through to 7.

'After the Sabbath was over, Mary Magdalene, Mary the mother of James, and Salome bought spices to go and annoint the body of Jesus. Very early on Sunday morning, at sunrise, they went to the tomb. On the way they said to one another, "Who will roll away the stone for us from the entrance to the tomb?" (It was a very large stone.)
Then they looked up and saw that the stone had already been rolled back. So they entered the tomb where they saw a young man sitting on the right, wearing a white robe – and they were alarmed.

DON'T BE ALARMED. I KNOW YOU ARE LOOKING FOR JESUS OF NAZARETH WHO WAS CRUCIFIED. HE IS NOT HERE. HE HAS BEEN RAISED! LOOK, HERE IS THE PLACE WHERE THEY PUT HIM. NOW GO AND GIVE THIS MESSAGE TO HIS DISCIPLES, INCLUDING PETER. HE IS GOING AHEAD OF YOU. THERE YOU WILL SEE HIM, JUST AS HE TOLD YOU.

Background info: It's now Sunday morning (Jesus had died on the Friday). Jesus had been buried in a tomb and a large round stone had been rolled in front of it. Added to that the Romans (with the encouragement of the religious leaders) had put a guard on the tomb to prevent the disciples from stealing the body and pretending that Jesus had come back to life again. They needn't have bothered. The disciples thought that that was the last they'd seen of Jesus and were pretty downcast.

Some questions for you: Why do you think Jesus had to come back to life again? Was it anything to do with proving that he really *was* God and that he'd successfully completed his mission?

I think Jesus needed to be raised back to life because:

And what would have been *your* reaction if *you'd* been one of the people who turned up at the tomb only to find that Jesus wasn't there?

My reaction would be:

Well, that's it for *this* **Agent Briefing**.

As you can see, checking out the Bible is an absolute **top priority** for *every* **agent of God**.

And don't forget, the enemy will try his **level best** to keep you away from this **essential agent manual**.

Okay, time for our last **Agent Briefing**.
For *this* one we've decided to keep your **code-cracking skills** on tip-top form. So that you don't need to keep whizzing back to the **Codecracker** on **page 80** we've done

you another one specially.
But *first*, a little bit of extra agent info for your interest.

Fascinating Fact:

The Romans weren't just good at building roads or conquering foreign lands. They were also pretty nifty when it came to devising cunning codes. One of them was the Polybius Code which works by writing down the Row number and then the Column number (instead of the letters). Have a go at the Polybius Code below.

COLUMNS

	1	2	3	4	5
1	A	B	C	D	E
2	F	G	H	I	J
3	K	L	M	N	O
4	P	Q	R	S	T
5	U	V	W	xy	Z

ROWS

Using the **Polybius Code** on the left see if you can finish off this well-known Bible Bit.
'Jesus called together his
45 53 15 32 52 15
14 24 44 13 24 41 32 15 44
together and gave them authority to drive out evil spirits and to heal every
14 24 44 15 11 44 15
and 44 24 13 31 34 15 44 44'

AGENT BRIEFING NUMBER EIGHT:
DO'S AND DON'TS

A *lot* of people seem to think that being an **agent of God** is all about what you *can't* do and how God's always trying to *spoil* your fun. Well, *this* **Agent Briefing** is here to **put the records straight**.

WHAT, YOU MEAN WE CAN DO WHAT WE LIKE? GREAT!

Er, that's not *quite* what I meant. What I *meant* is that loads of people think that **God** is just one **big party-pooper** and signing up to be a Christian is going to be the end of life as you know it. Well, for starters that just a load of **nonsense** but the second thing is that God *has* given us **rules and laws** to live by.

Why's he done that?

Well certainly **not** to give us a hard time.
In fact it's the complete *opposite*.

SEARCH ME?!

God wants the very *best* for every single person that he's *ever* made, but because *he* made us *he* knows what's good (and what's bad) for us. All the rules and stuff are just there to keep us **safe** and to make sure life goes **well** for us.

Just imagine for one *mad* moment there were no rules or laws...

Hmm! *That's* not going to work is it?

If we all did just what *we* wanted then it would be **absolute chaos**.

That's why God's given us some very sensible rules to follow and to make our lives go well.

The Bible's *full* of all different kinds of rules and regulations but the ones that we're gonna check out are called the

'**Ten Commandments**' and they were given by **God** to a guy called **Moses** (at the top of a mountain, if you're interested). They were written down on **two slabs of stone** (just so Moses wouldn't forget them I suppose).

Using your **Codecracker** you've gotta out work what each of these rules from God *are*. Over to *you* Moses!

CODECRACKER

A B C D E F G H I J K L M N
Z Y X W V U T S R Q P O N M

O P Q R S T U V W X Y Z
L K J I H G F E D C B A

How did you get on? Just in case you had any blips here are the answers ...

1) DON'T WORSHIP ANY OTHER GOD'S BUT GOD HIMSELF
2) DON'T PUT PEOPLE OR THINGS BEFORE GOD
3) DON'T USE GOD'S NAME AS A SWEAR WORD
4) REST FOR ONE DAY EACH WEEK AND MAKE IT A SPECIAL DAY TO WORSHIP GOD
5) SHOW YOUR PARENTS RESPECT AND GOD WILL GIVE YOU A LONG LIFE
6) DON'T MURDER ANYONE OR EVEN HATE ANYONE
7) ONLY HAVE SEX WITH THE PERSON YOU ARE MARRIED TO
8) DON'T STEAL SOMEONE ELSE'S BELONGINGS
9) DON'T TELL LIES OR MAKE UNTRUE ACCUSATIONS
10) DON'T BE JEALOUS OF WHAT OTHER PEOPLE HAVE AND THEN WANT IT FOR YOURSELF

Well, it looks like the end of this book is in sight but there's a few *more* things do do *before* we wrap it up.

One of the most *important* things you've gotta know (and we've said it already) is that God's got a **totally amazing plan for your life**.

But even *more* amazing is the fact that *you* are a **one-off**. Try as you might, you'll not find another person on planet earth exactly like *you*.

The *big* question is...

Here's how.

First off you need to get back to being friends with God. If you haven't done this yet then Boring Bible book *Crazy Christians* will tell you how.

Then you need to spend a bit of time **communicating with HQ** – but not just chatting all the time – do some *listening* as well. The *main* plan God has for your life is for you to get to know him better, but the *other* big plan is all that **agent of God** stuff about telling people about Jesus and being an *effective* agent. As you stick close to your **Boss** he'll start to reveal (bit by bit) some of the brilliant things that he's got lined up for you so you don't need to rush around like a **headless chicken** trying to make things happen ...

So, **ease up**, **trust God** and everything'll fall into place at just the **right time**.

And one last thing to download and store in your agent memory banks is that God chose **you** – you didn't choose *him*. *That* means that when he **handpicked you** to sign up as one of his agents he already knew *exactly* what he had planned for your life. Is that good or what?!

Now *before* we go our separate ways I'm going to set you some special **agent of God missions** to carry out.

Are you up for it?

Here goes ...

AGENT OF GOD MISSION: ONE...

Forgive...Forgive...Forgive...

Your *first* mission, young agent of God (should you choose to accept it) is probably one of the hardest missions you will *ever* be given but we at mission control believe that you are able (with power from God) to complete it **successfully**.

First **select your target** – someone who has let you down, said something horrid to you or hurt you in some way or another. Have you thought of someone?

Now, you can see why we said it was gonna be a bit of a **toughie**. The thing is, Jesus said that unless we forgive other people the shutters stay down between us and God.

Why's that? Simple.

The Bible says that even though *we've* all done wrong to God, *he* was still prepared to take the punishment for it *all* so that *we* could be forgiven. If *we've* been forgiven loads by *God* then *we* shouldn't hang about when it comes to forgiving *other* people.

Just in case you're not convinced, check out this story that Jesus told to prove the point ...

'Once there was a king who decided to check on his servants' accounts. He had just begun to do so when one of them was brought in who owed him millions of pounds ...

The king felt sorry for him so he forgave him the debt and let him go. Then the man went out and met one of his fellow servants who owed him a few pounds ...

But he refused and instead had him thrown into jail until he paid the debt. When the other servants saw what had happened they were upset and went to the king and told him everything. So the king called in the servant ...

So the king sent the servant to jail to be punished until he paid back the whole amount.'

So, as you can see, **Jesus**, (God's *No.1* agent) says that *not* forgiving someone is a **big no-no**. That's because God's agents are meant to be like their Boss in the way they carry out their agent of God activities. Because God's forgiven *us*, then *we* forgive others. **End of story!**

Right, have you you thought of someone you need to forgive? Great.

Okay, here's what you're gonna need to do.

First, say these words to God and include the name of the person you're forgiving...

> DEAR GOD, JUST LIKE YOU HAVE FORGIVEN ME, I WANT TO FORGIVE
>
> ....
> (Name of person)

Now the thing to remember is that you don't need to actually *feel* anything to forgive someone. What they did or said to you might still hurt you, but as an **agent of God** *you* have **God's power** to make a **decision** to forgive them anyway.

Boring Bible Top Tip: Ask God to take away the pain of any hurt they have caused you. He can now do that because you've made the first move to forgive. And you don't *even* need to tell the person face to face that you've forgiven them (not unless you want to) – that's just between *you* and *God*!

Once you've completed Mission One, fill in the Mission One Done! box.

MISSION ONE

DONE!

put a tick in the white box

Let's move on to your *next* mission, young agent of God.

AGENT OF GOD MISSION: TWO...

Others First...Others First...

Your second mission is *another* one that's going to push you to you limits as an agent of God.

For the next **24 hours** you've gotta put **other people first**.

What exactly does that *mean*? Let me show you ...

Or how about something like *this* ...

Getting the picture?

That's good. But *why* is putting other people **first** such a big deal for **agents of God**?

Here's why.

The whole reason human beings ever turned their backs on the chance to be friends with God, way back at the beginning of time (check out Boring Bible book *Ballistic Beginnings*), was 'cos they wanted **their own way**. *They* wanted to be **No.1**. And *that* was where things went wrong. Check out a bit from the Bible to discover what *Jesus* says about **putting others first**.

'Jesus and his disciples were having supper. Jesus rose from the table, took off his outer garment and tied a towel round his waist. Then he poured some water into a basin and began to wash his disciples' feet and dry them with the towel ...

... said one of the disciples called Simon Peter.

After Jesus had washed their feet he put his outer garment back on and returned to the table.

Then Jesus said...

Just in case you're a little bit confused, Jesus *wasn't* saying that we've got to go round washing everyone's feet ...

What he *meant* was that just like *he* served his disciples (even though he was their *master*) we've gotta look for ways to serve other people – which means **putting them first**.

Now I *did* say that this was just a **24 hour mission** but that was only to encourage you to get started.

But being an **agent of God** means that putting other people first is something you *should* be doing doing **24:7** (24 hours a day: 7 days a week).

Once you've successfully completed your *first* 24 hour mission tick the Mission Two Done! box and then just **keep going**.

And don't forget to communicate with HQ (pray) when you're finding it a bit hard going.

Your **Boss in heaven** will dispatch **immediate power** (the Holy Spirit) to give you a fresh boost of determination to keep this mission **active**.

MISSION TWO
DONE!

put a tick in the white box

More Boring Bible Agent Jokes:

What do secret agents keep as pets?
Spy-ders!

Why did the secret agent call a plumber when his phone wasn't working?

Because there was a **tap** on it!

AGENT OF GOD MISSION: THREE...

Clean Up...Clean Up...Clean Up...

Before you even *think* it, this isn't another mission about washing feet or for that matter *any* sort of household chores. Nope, what this *last* mini-mission is to do with is something called '**Holiness**'. (Sounds scary doesn't it?)

Before you quickly skip past this mission how about if I fill you in with some info that'll put your mind at rest?

The Bible says that **Christians** (agents of God) have got to live **holy** lives, just like God does, (and it's *his* example we're all following, right?). All being *holy* means is **being different**. Different from *what* you may ask?
Check out the next page and you'll find out ...

Being Different Means...

Not this...

But this...

Not this...

But this...

Not this...

But this...

So what *God* expects from his agents is for us to **clean up** our lives and be **different**. *That* way you'll start to make a difference in the big, wide world as an **agent of God**.

Why not check out some of the things that you're doing and if you think that they don't match up to what *God* expects, then do something about it. For starters, think of just **one thing** that could get cleaned up in your life and when you have done something about it, tick it off in the Mission Three Done! box.

MISSION TWO
DONE!

put a tick in
the white box

Well, that's just about it for *this* Boring Bible book.

I hope you've found it helpful to get you up and running as an **effective agent of God**.

And as you'll have discovered as you've put your agent powers to the test investigating this book ... being a Christian is definitely **not for wimps!**

BUT WHAT ABOUT COLLECTING POSTAGE STAMPS?

Oh, alright then.
I give in.
Stamp collecting
isn't for wimps
either.
Happy?

SURE AM! SO CAN I SHOW YOU MY COLLECTION NOW? HEY! WHY'S EVERYONE LEAVING?

And now for the moment you've all been waiting for...

Why This Book is Called 'Saints Alive!'

The reason this Boring Bible book is called '**Saints Alive!**'...

... is because *every* Christian is actually called a '**Saint**' (according to the Bible). *Most* people think that a saint is some sort of special person who's been dead for hundreds and hundreds of years – **but not so!**

Which means that *you*, young agent of God, are a **saint** and also one who's very much **alive**.

So *that's* why this book is called '**Saints Alive!**' 'cos God's saints (like you and me) are meant to be **alive and kicking**, getting stuck into all the exciting missions that God has lined up for us. **There you have it!**